AF414159

The Blessings

poems
by Gus Speth

The Blessings

poems

by Gus Speth

www.watershedpublications.org

The Blessings
Poems
©2022 Gus Speth

ISBN: 979-8-21810-124-4

Cover art by the author
Design/production, Anne Pace

Printed in the United States
November 2022

Dearest in Memory
Amelia and Gus
Mom and Dad

Contents

**On the last day of the world,
I would want to plant a tree.**

W.S. Merwin

Really Human

Are you really a human?
How do you know you're not a robot?
By spotting stoplights in an online matrix?
Better, hum a little Chopin,
wade barefoot in the ice cold surf,
pick up a shell (a Lettered Olive!),
imagine the old rocks are a chorten
and circle it slowly clockwise,
laugh back at the Laughing Gulls,
hold a hand, smell her hair,
remember her at childbirth.

Adagio

The sun that day burst bright
orange through the trees
and settled on Lee's sleepy face.

Emily was gone already,
away to fix breakfast for Maud,
95 and bright as that sun.

The dogs waited, restless for him.
They loved and teased in equal dose.
His pup took off with his old socks.

Lee had some coffee and corn flakes
with blueberries from lord knows where.
They ate the ones he somehow dropped.

The yard, now green, was full of Robins.
Bluebirds had claimed their little homes.
Maybe they were born there last year.

He sat on the front porch and read
the Times online, and did Wordle.
He realized he still liked Ike.

There were a ton of new emails.
He did his day's inbox triage,
checked on the war in brave Ukraine.

A doe with fawns suddenly appeared.
Just as quickly, nothing was there.
So quietly the dogs missed them.

He saw the swing in the basswood.
The grandkids loved that swing.
They no longer needed pushes.

He filled the bird feeders full up.
They're back—red, blue, yellow, and black!
He'd learned so much watching them.

Lee was content, but then was stirred.
He had a thought he'd had before—
about magic in what is commonplace,
about the ordinary grace of everyday.

Me and 80 and You

I am entering old age today.
I know you think it was earlier,
back when you gave away my golf clubs
and borrowed a walker for me.
Well, in any case I am 80 today.
It is surely a milestone, but
marking what I am not certain.
Do I now become a Wise Old Man?
or a wizened old curmudgeon?
At least: a smoke signal announcing to all that
the Dark Knight has arrived on a nearby hill.

I have lived through a third of America.
A mere three spans of 80
takes us back to the Founding.
I remember from Truman forward,
or has it been backwards?
A kaleidoscope of joy and tragedy,
and far too much of it tragedy.
The climate destruction,
the desperate poverty and discrimination,
it is sometimes too much to bear.

After a long lifetime of
working hard for good causes,
I wonder with what result.
I think the reality is that
I've mostly been along for the ride,
a pimple on the butt of Progress.
But have I succeeded at trying?
That's not enough, but it is something.
Now it's time for me to move on,
and I am finding it hard to let go.

When asked the source of happiness
and urged to state the matter simply,
the psychologist replied, "Other people."
I can vouch for that. I celebrate
my many friends and comrades. Still,
one other person has been central to me
over this long journey of a happy life.
From high school to this memorable day,
despite the golf clubs, the missing chain saw,
that person is the wonderful you.

What Did They Know?

Those who knew are mostly gone.
But what was it that they knew?
How to jigger fish along the riverbank.
How to diagram a sentence.
When fields were full of Bobolinks.

The small flat-bottom boat glided slowly along the
bank of the easygoing black water. Gene, the paddler,
lived a modest life in the down and out town. He drank
too much and smoked too much and ate too little, but
nobody paddled with his grace and skill. Moving the
wooden boat quietly under the overhang, he positioned
it perfectly for the old fisherman in the front to jigger his
cane pole gently so that the three tiny hooks tied close
to the pole and their crickets excited the redbreasts and
bream into striking, an offer they could not and did not
refuse. The men were thankful for a good catch and for
a good river and thankful too for the black snake staying
quietly in the overhang. They joked about the fisherman
who panicked when one dropped into the bottom of his
boat and he shot it.

Miss Higgins taught high school English, or so it was
called, but it was grammar, and a rigorous, demanding
version of grammar it was. Over a career of several
decades she began each class by striding to the
blackboard and revealing the proper diagramming
of the sentence she had assigned to her students as
homework. She offered a prize to students who could
properly diagram the first sentence of *Silas Marner*.
During the year her students learned about adjectives

attributive, predicate, and appositive, and more on
appositives and predicate nominatives, gerunds and
noun infinitives, voice and mood. Spelling, punctuation,
and proper forms of polite address and usage were
not overlooked. There were hundreds of rules to be
learned, and they were. Her students would never be
thought to be the hicks they seemed to many. They
would understand that there is a right way and a wrong
way and that in life as in grammar some things are
improper. To Miss Higgins good grammar showed self-
respect and, even more important, respect for others.

The Way to know the Bobolink
From every other Bird
Precisely as the Joy of him —
Obliged to be inferred.

Emily Dickinson's fields and meadows must have been
full of Bobolinks. Indeed, they make appearances in
over twenty of her poems — her irreverent, rowdy
sorcerers of the meadow with their napes of cream and
bubbling song. She wrote of her sadness when these
dear little blackbirds were gone, but back then she was
noticing their departure — down through Florida,
across the Gulf, and on to where winter is summer.
Today, Bobolinks are departing, but departing very
differently. Populations are down sixty percent since
1970. Destroy the habitat and you destroy the birds, and
Bobolinks, Larks and other meadow birds are in steep
decline. So, will our children one day ask what we did,
or didn't do, to save the fields of Bobolinks?

What the Preacher Saw

Looking up, he saw the bluebird sky
and the Ben & Jerry's clouds,
the hills moving gently to the woods
sparkling now with last night's snow.

Two tall pines rising above
the stick bare branches
of maple, ash, and beech
atop Morrill Mountain's ridge.

Silhouetted phthalo green
against that crisp blue sky,
the pines seemed a pair, together.
The preacher paused.

The pine on the left rounded,
perhaps shaped by lightning.
The other a rising spire
leaning leftward, leftward

as if reaching over
to whisper or be near.
A steady wind can do that, but
he thought something more.

Sunday Morning Coming Down

I cannot hear "Sunday Mornin' Comin' Down"
without recalling how one Sunday morning
I was studying for the bar exam in DC and
not wanting to tackle negotiable instruments
I took a walk down the sleeping city sidewalk
that ran through my diverse neighborhood
black and white poor and not poor cheek to jowl
and how at that point I wanted to work eventually
for the Children's Defense Fund and represent
those on the losing side of that unequal equation
and I walked past where a black woman was
sitting on her front steps as her two kids
played on the curb and sidewalk
and I smiled at her and she said
"What you laughing at, white boy?
Something funny to you? You ain't here."
I kept walking lest there was more coming
but shaken I kept saying to myself
blunder blunder blunder blunder boy
did you not see that she was real and
you were just a character in your dream?

The Gazette

We old people think we have
earned the right to be heard!
To have a respectful audience!
The young editors think
we had our chance, and muffed it.

My friend, also eighty, well, he
thinks that that is ageism.
He has written some letters
to the names on the masthead,
thus showing his age for sure.

So the battle is joined between
the forces of old age wisdom
and youth's fresh perspective.
The scene's set for compromise,
but no one's in a mood for that!

It's not really a fair fight.
Those whippersnappers
have seized the high ground—
the jobs once ours now held
by ever younger kids.

My friend and I decided to
have some drinks instead.
And at some point that evening
We rambled onto the idea of
The Geezer Gazette.

We'd gather in the has beens—
old guys and gals still with fire.
We played with some slogans:
"The Wisdom of the Aged"
"ALL THE NEWS THAT FITS BIG PRINT."
"Wisdom! Experience! …Wisdom!"
  (or did I say that?)

We dreamed of working again
with writers who'd earned their spurs,
who'd started out covering sports
and recalled Scotty Reston's quip:
"I don't know what I think
until I read what I've written."

The *Gazette* would have a special
Department of Endless Edits,
staffed by the most crotchety
for submissions from those under 50.
Youngsters would start as cub reporters
assigned to cover peach pageants and parades.

The evening ended, a short drive home
lost in my memories of waiting for
the morning papers, sure to find there
my latest Op Ed filled with optimism
and the rambunctiousness of youth.

Voices

While the peepers perfume the twilight air
and the barred owl sings her simple song,
we rock gently, slowly on the old porch and
in the gathering darkness listen for voices.

Who, who speaks for you? Who speaks for you?

For the longest forever it was Mother.
I hear her now at dawn, helping with
homework I was too tired for last night.
Where would I be if she were not there,
and now here on the sofa beside me?

Who, who speaks for you? Who speaks for you?

Dad is a ragamuffin, a mop of happy gray hair,
a jokester who keeps running the soft
soothing patter of simple laughter.
He tells the Principal he will keep me straight
and military school will not be necessary.

Who, who speaks for you? Who speaks for you?

Time evaporates with the peepers and slow rocking.
I am back at the beginning, and I hear another voice.
Don't worry, Miss Amelia, you got a fine boy.
He'll be something one day, I know it.

Who, who speaks for you? Who speaks for you?

There have been so many who spoke for me,
voices heard now over the transom of evening.
All along the river of my life, there have been
angels who spoke kind words on my behalf.

Who, who speaks for you? Who speaks for you?

Reverie

Dangling emotions, residue of dreams,
orphaned feeling now attached to nothing.
They linger longer as the years pile up,
while memories rush about, fresh as life.
He studies grains of sugar sparkling in the spoon,
all destined to dissolve in coffee he drinks too often.
He recalls the many friends he has had and lost
through decades of changing jobs and distant locations.
They were almost all good people, honorable and
doing hard work to make the world a bit better.
A wave of gratitude and affection warms him.
He thinks of the blessing and joy they were to him—
how they were the clear water in which he swam.
It has been so terribly long.
Faces he once knew now drift in front of him.
He would like to know what became of them
and hopes they moved happily into their futures.
He hopes too that they remembered him fondly,
and he knows that is all he can ever ask.

Going Crazy

For years I tried to be
calm, sane, and reasonable.
I thought that was the path
to being highly credible.

"We'll save the world, if our
approach is non-threatening.
Persuasion is the key," I said
to co-workers who were listening.

"Businessmen will hear us,
and politicians too.
They will take our advice,
and then will follow through."

But it didn't work out that way.
We find ourselves today
in a sad, troubled place
with the world in disarray.

Events, we see, are shaped
by those unhinged from reality,
moved by mindless angsts,
who shout to force us to agree.

So I have been at work lately
to become a lot like crazy.
I work at it every day;
it's not a task for the lazy.

The aim of my new project is
changing my whole modality.
When I'm carrying on plum crazy,
perhaps I too can shape reality!

A Nearby Place

George remembered what old Doc,
summoning his most ferocious,
had commanded him never to forget:
We are all Christ, Doc insisted,
and we are all crucified.

He remembered it when
he learned that Johanna and Karl
had to sell their beloved farm,
the one up on Orion Brook,
to cover the damn taxes.

It came to him when Jennifer,
who composed exquisite music
mostly for string quartets,
found years of work in ashes
but, mercy, her baby unharmed.

He recalled what Doc said when
a college prof, his dear friend,
was quietly bypassed for tenure,
his politics too radical and
his religion too atheistic.

But most clearly he remembered it when
he was at the prof's home the night
a local quartet played a piece by Jennifer
composed to honor all the many contributions
Johanna and Karl had made to their town.

The News Knows Its Audience

The big-time reporters have gone home.
The foreign pols have visited,
walked around the crumbled cities.
They too are safely home now.
Months into Russia's invasion,
it's time for the news to move on!

There's another shooting in Texas!
Or is it Illinois? Or Florida?
Time to shift the cameras there.
Top pols are there now.
Wall to wall coverage, please.
Interview the grieving parents.
Do a little dance around gun control.
The viewers will then feel better.

Need some less depressing news?
Switch to a courtroom drama, somewhere!
Maybe even Russia.
Or to a British scandal. There's always one.
If all else fails, bring on the glurge.

Hey, news guys, sorry for that sarcasm.
But is social media ruining our kids?
Are we living in a plutocracy,
crippling poverty and social insecurity
surrounding a bunch of billionaires
buying up everything? Even space.
Is there still an opioids crisis?
A famine in the Horn of Africa?
And, oh,
do we really need your sponsors' stuff?

I know, that's too much negative.
But you report our pols telling us
America is the shining city on the hill.
We can do anything we put our minds to.
We are the land of opportunity.
We are the last best hope.
I am still moved by the rhetoric—
but chilled now by the reality.

We Awoke Together

She dreamed she wore a dress.
I asked if she were sure.
"Yes," she said, "a dress no less,
the picture of demure."

"Were you a young girl,
or dreaming what's to be?"
"I wore earrings of pearl.
The 50s I'd say," said she.

The past unfurls,
good memories rush in:
Such a beautiful girl,
now and way back then.

It was in 1958
when we first fell in love.
Behind the high school gate,
first kisses from above.

And kisses ever since,
in love through many times.
I was not so very dense
I missed the many rhymes.

Her life has been a wonder,
a joy that spread to me.
Decades now to ponder
how blessed my life can be.

"Come beside me, dear one,"
I ask of her just then.
"Kiss me in this morning sun.
Let's once again begin."

Hopium

It takes a lot of hopium
to get me through the day.
There is always more hopium,
and I will take it any way.

I can grow my own hopium.
My mind's a fertile field.
The less I know, the more I grow.
You cannot beat that deal.

I got a bumper crop last year
when I turned off the news.
Being hopeful was easy when
I took a long news snooze.

There are far worse addictions;
hopium just affects the mind.
Yet in terms of climate worries,
it leaves them far behind.

Dreamy hope, comforting hope,
whenever needed it's there.
There's always more hopium
when I'm in my easy chair.

Hope without costs,
hope without consequence,
this hope's a dope's dope
in a cauldron of innocence.

The Difference

Hope is putting seeds into the ground.
Hopium is expecting the garden to be fine without you.

Hope is trying to sing in tune.
Hopium is believing it happened.

Hope is a kick in the butt.
Hopium is an easy chair.

Hope is "in the shadows,
in the people who are inventing the world
while no one looks." (Solnit)
Hopium is just looking.

Hope says "cannabis is safe."
Hopium says "tobacco too!"

Hope is wanting tomorrow to be better than today.
Hopium is counting on it.

Hope is shouting at the TV.
Hopium is thinking somebody hears you.

Hope is writing a poem.
Hopium is believing it will be published.

Hope is making cornbread stuffing.
Hopium is thinking it won't taste like cornbread.

Hope is taking supplements.
Hopium is taking supplements.

Love Song

I want to be a singer songwriter
Make a great song for you
Can't think of anything better
Than making a song for you

I listened to music last night
Brought back the old dreams
Me being a singer songwriter
But damn, it's harder than it seems

You're in my head now
But the words don't come soon
Gotta get it right, try as I might
I'm still looking for the tune

It's been a long, long time
Since I sat down with my guitar
What I learned back then
It was a bridge too far

Singer songwriter is harder
When you can't sing a note
That's another of my problems
Even when its words I wrote

I want to be a singer songwriter
Make a great song for you
Can't think of anything better
Than making a song for you

I'll never be a singer songwriter
Can't write, can't play, can't sing
But I know how much you love me
So it doesn't mean a thing

The Longest History

We do not exist
because we think.
We exist
and then we think.
Our minds are
but our bodies
doing special work
and our bodies are
but stardust
now folded together
by eons of evolution.
The universe has a story
and we are part of it.
That story is now
telling us that
we are the universe
looking back on itself,
contemplating its reality.
The universe has
become aware.

There Once Was a ...

There once was a woman named Jane.
She spoke out, so some men thought her a pain.
On Choice, she ramped up the decibels to double,
and she gave six Justices big trouble.
She won when Roe was law once again.

⦿⦿

There was once a character named Corning
who worked on his poems each morning.
He always found things to adjust.
Over words he would endlessly fuss.
He said his poems were all still aborning.

⦿⦿

There was a young woman from Perth
who had been waltzing almost since birth.
One exciting night found Matilda
dancing arm in arm with a lovely Sarah.
Together they floated far above earth.

⦿⦿

There once was a judge named Beau.
He'd fix tickets and more just so.
The cops laid a trap
but he was gone in a snap.
Beau was last seen in Acapulco.

I am thinking it's past time for bed,
but bed is what I now dread.
It's something I wish I'd forgot:
that I have so many trips to the pot.
But I can find nothing in its stead.

∞

Jan was striving for poetry,
and she worked quite hard for drollery.
But her phrases fell flat some times,
and she had trouble with her rhymes.
Her big soul saved her from obscurity.

∞

Lucas sat down to write a lim'rick.
He deployed a many a gimmick.
Luke thought he was quite clever,
but his wife murmured "never."
So he closed his tablet, heartsick.

With a Name Like That

Many years ago
my wife Cameron and I
went to a spot in New Orleans
in the Marigny district
along Frenchmen Street.
Summer Reyes was there
singing beautifully with her band,
and I said to Cameron,
"You are as good as Summer
and if I were your manager
and you had a name like Summer Reyes,
wow, we could really go places,
touring around and having fun."

Named Gus as I am, I'm
sensitive to these matters.
A friend in the UN once said
"You become your name."
Movies love Gus — for animals.
Soon I will be a mule or mouse.
It has occurred to me
that if I were instead named
Jonathan Countryman,
I might have made a
good life in politics.

Old Sam's Story

Did you know Molly?
It was new summer's day,
bright and fresh that morning,
and she was in the garden
with her favorite flowers budding.
How she loved her roses,
almost as much as I loved her.
Now this longest day returns,
and she is gone.

The sunset brings shadows
to untended blooms.
Bluebirds pause and float
from post to ground.
Everybody knew Molly!
And they loved her too.
She was a woman in full,
if I may say that.
She would look you in the eye
and you were in that moment
everything to her.
Her daddy once said of her
"Lord, Molly, you can charm
the lard out of a biscuit."
She charmed me every day.
And on this endless day,
she is gone.

(continued)

Itching is between
the hurt and its healing,
and I am itching all over.
The loss of her surrounds me.
I am covered by memories
of her silver hair on my shoulder.
On this day she would have loved,
she is gone.

Somewhere Lovely

What Heaven was ever made
but as beauty wrought in sun and shade?

Jonathan Countryman sat on his porch
in Litchfield Beach in the late afternoon.
He had just finished his fifth and his last
term as state senator and was thinking.
Half into his Bloody Mary, he knew
he had accomplished some important things,
but not as much as he had hoped at the start.
He became a leader of the progressives,
but this was South Carolina after all.
That damn flag yet flies around the state.
But I am still vertical, he thought,
still vertical despite it all.

On that warm March day, Jennifer joined him.
Married for fifty-one years come July,
she knew what he was thinking, and she said,
"It was worth it. We made a difference.
Even if we didn't, it was still worth it.
All the effort, all the trying…beautiful!
We should go out and celebrate. Tonight.
Somewhere lovely."

Jonathan had heard about a new place,
a casual restaurant that seemed perfect.
Most nights they had a band playing.
It was near Murrells Inlet up the beach,
so they made reservations and took off.

When they got there, the thing they noticed
were the grounds — the beautiful landscaping.
The camellias were blooming pink and red.
An old man was bent over the roses,
clipping them expertly to get the best.
Jennifer was a good gardener herself,
and he started talking roses with her.
"My apartment is down the road from here.
I volunteered to care for this garden.
My name is Sam. My wife Molly loved roses
and when I work here, I remember all
the good things with her. It is a blessing."

The restaurant was indeed lovely.
She's an attractive woman, Jonathan thought,
as they were warmly greeted at the door.
"Hello," she said, "and welcome to our place.
I'm Sally. I know about your service,
and I have admired it from afar.
Thank you for all you have done!
This restaurant is something my husband
and I have long wanted, and here we are.
That's him over there where they are cooking
the best food on the coast, or so we claim!"

Jonathan could see an animated man
with curly gray hair busy in the kitchen.
To his surprise he was communicating
with the kitchen crew using sign language.
"He's overcome everything life offered,"
Sally said. "This is our daughter, Fairhope.
She will show you to your table."

As for Cameron and Gus, well, they were
at a corner table eating crab cakes,
taking in the whole scene with pleasure.
To their delight, they had noticed that
Summer Reyes would be coming soon.
They would be back.

The Reckoning

The shadow moves across
the void of moral reckoning.

It blocks light,
light vanishes.
It shreds truth,
truth vanishes.
It crushes hope,
hope vanishes.

Darkness gathers
in hate, ignorance,
violence.
It knows
no delight or joy.
It sees no beauty.

Will there be a reckoning?
A confrontation with evil?
There is a pause, then
one community says yes
and soon many others,
for there are still
domains of truth
shafts of bright light
people of great hope,
weary but brave
and alive in the world.

Fishing with the Family

There once was a boat that the salesman said
was solely owned by the preacher.
"He used it on Sundays after church
to take out his wife, the teacher."
Out on charming Chincoteague Bay

I remember it all with a sense of dread.
Every last word that salesman said
went straight into my gullible head.
Embarrassment can still turn me red.
Out on charming Chincoteague Bay

Never buy a new boat or an old motor,
that's the sage advice from my father.
I could have listened a great deal better
and thus greatly reduced my bother.
Out on charming Chincoteague Bay

The motor died early one Sunday
fishing with my family that day
far out in Chincoteague Bay.
The good news is, I'm pained to say,
the Coast Guard was not too far away.
Out on charming Chincoteague Bay

Leroy's Lament

I sit here working crosswords
dripping black coffee on my dog,
trying not to think of you,
watching this morning's fog.

We had such a time together,
but now you're really gone.
I need four letters down
and I can't but think of "torn."

I thought if I were drunk again
it would be easier for me to tell.
So I chugged a pint of Jim Beam.
That made you mad as hell.

I was trying to explain
my running around didn't matter.
I said she was just off and on,
but that just made you madder.

You left two months ago
right after that big fight.
If I hadn't hit so hard,
would we still be alright?

I'm glad you didn't call the cops.
You could have put me deep in it.
I guess I should be thanking you —
one more, I wouldn't be acquitted.

I got my smokes, JB, and dog.
And I'm getting use to feeling sorry.
I think about having you back.
Perhaps one day that still will be.

Dream on, lover boy,
you worthless pile of it.
After too long a spell with you,
it's way past time I split.

Consider the Leaders

BBC said world leaders are havering.
Over here, that word is, well, napoo.
Yet, truly, havering may be
better than being decisive.
Consider who are the leaders!
Some leaders we prefer vacillating,
procrastinating, murmurating.
We will celebrate their prudence,
circumspection, and their caution,
sometimes even declaring it wisdom
and meriting a nice vacation.

Where the World Is Local
(Rural Edition)

Mailboxes are used for many things, plus mail.
The postman just smiles.

The town store will take a message.
"Please remind her to bring some mortadella home."

Cars stop in the road to chat.
The other cars wait and don't blow.

Folks ask about our dogs by name.
Just like they were our children.

There are no secrets.
Except where to find morels.

Big box stores are kept out of our area!
Shoppers head to the strip mall across the state line.

Our dear Mamie, living at home, is 98.
There's a sign-up sheet for visits with her.

It is a mistake to close the blinds.
It just makes folks suspicious.

The neighbors' garden is an embarrassment.
It embarrasses me every time I see mine.

The Promise

the snow's just gone, the moment feels unreal
the earth is pat down gray and brown
a porcupine moves slowly through our field
headed somewhere between lost and found

nothing too dramatic going on
so much of life seeming gone
spring held in check again
spates of warming asking when
left bears and sap turning round
wondering do I now head up or down

I saw a sugar house last night
late but all cranked up despite
bright and busy with the boiling
beer and banter slake the toiling
these times worth remembering

climate change is messing with the season
messing too with plain reason
the climate models are predicting
that maples will be disappearing
what's left, what's green we must hold tight
no, not going gently without a fight

The Six Seasons of New England

Greening

is the beginning of everything,
the eternal return.
Explosions of chartreuse
a dozen shades,
lime and light green,
but ephemeral.
Crocuses poke up,
daffodils show their faces,
nature waking up.
Sap made it to your waffles.
A season of reassurance.

Garden

means work, so much to do.
Days long and warm,
growing season short.
Everyone busy—
setting out the garden,
tedding the hay,
putting up the dilly beans,
hoping for good weather.
Bluebirds reclaim their houses.
Baseball and no school.
A season of sustenance.

Foliage

is a harlequin duck,
impossible not to watch.
Colors joyous, playful.
Nature's grace,
free, bountiful, undeserved.
Ample old barns, orchards,
fat sheep, dwarf Nigerian goats,
county fairs with
draft horse pulls and pig races,
blues and bluegrass.
A season of worship.

Stick

peaks in November.
Everything visible, exposed.
The land lies open.
It lacks color
but adds contour.
Stubble fields where
once grew hay and corn.
A thousand snow geese
feed in the Addison marshes.
There is a nip in the wind,
and snow on Camel's Hump.
A season of seeing.

Snow

seems forever.
Pumping the brakes won't
stop the slide into the ditch.
Before COVID, cabin fever.
Yet for many, snow makes
this place the joy that it is:
maple limbs dappled white,
snowmobile trails snake
through woods, crossing Nordic ones,
black diamond slopes awaiting.
Time for reading.
A season of contemplation.

Mud

is the dreaded one,
the curse on all
who use dirt roads,
and here that is everyone.
Let's hear no more
of "mud, glorious mud":
the mud is where cars sink to the axles.
Mud is a rite of passage,
mercifully short,
something that must be crossed
to find the Greening.
A season of anticipation.

In a Dry Land

My TV tuned to the January 6 Hearings,
I hear reports tearing my heart apart.
But through the window above the TV
the hummingbirds dart about their feeders.
Tiny things, they seem ferocious today.
A ruby-red throat glistens in the PM sun.
In the distance giant maples and ash bow
to a new wind promising rain in a dry land.
As it begins with a low growl of thunder,
I go to the porch for a better view.
A dark and dense purple gray moves in,
occupying every foot of available sky.
It's going to be a powerful storm,
cleansing, the one we have been awaiting.

Ice Would Be Nice

Expect the end of the world!
What, then, a flood?
Or will it be fire?
As you might inspire,
Frost said ice,
ice would suffice.
But expect the end of ice.
Without a market price
there is no future for ice.
And even with a price,
Warming has shaved the dice.
Now, I wouldn't swear an oath,
but on fire or flood, I'd say both.

What Do You Want To Be?

This tale of a young man's fancy
begins in a small Southern town.
It ends in south Chicago,
an early aspiration in tatters.

He wanted to go into politics
thought it would be interesting
and keep his growing ego happy.
He thought he might go far.

His first job, in high school,
tacking posters on poles.
He can't remember for whom.
His work lined the highways.

Then, in college, a summer job
working for his DC congressman.
Assigned to write right-wing speeches,
it should have cured him.

In 1968 he became Gene McCarthy's
campaign coordinator for his state.
At the infamous 1968 Chicago convention,
he secured but one vote for Clean Gene.

It's been said Chicago was a gas.
He was tear gassed there, protesting.
With no pass, Mayor Daley's thugs
hustled him off the convention floor.

He realized he wasn't in touch—
he and his base drifting apart.
The thought of chasing that base
cured him of politics for good.

Signs can appear telling us which
dreams to hold to and which to let go.
He is glad he saw that sign back then.
But he still wants to be President.

Embrace of the Virus

Bring your own wine to communion!
That's the day's COVID commandment.
Someone said don't breathe on the cheese.
This thing has made fools of us.
Haven't we had enough already?

So, after my fourth injection,
I put up my masks,
ventured out into the big world,
and gave some hugs.
Next thing I knew I was wrapped in the
feverish embrace of a new Omicron, and
wondering who breathed on the cheese.

In the Neighborhood

My neighbor is dying of cancer at an early age;
I am healthy as I tumble and stagger past eighty.

My neighbor's only child was killed in Iraq;
my children are fine, the parents of six.

My neighbor's husband lost most memories;
my wife provides companionship every day.

I have benefitted from white privilege;
my neighbor has long suffered discrimination.

My neighbor cannot make ends meet;
I have a comfortable retirement nest egg.

My neighbor is depressed by disappointments;
mine are real too but don't lay me low.

Neither I nor my neighbors did anything much
to deserve or merit our divergent situations.
Life's blessings fall unfairly, rather randomly.
Here's nonsense: people get what they deserve.

Our job, then, in every way we can, is
to work to bring fairness forward,
to defy fate with neighborliness.

The hopes we can make happen
in lives connected close by caring
are all the light we ever need.

What We Know, and Don't

If God is out there, here are some things we know:

1.   **God is full of energy.** Everyone knows about the Big Bang of energy that kicked things off, but even the tiny subatomic particles like quarks and electrons are points of energy. Almost everything is energy. God can even make energy happen in a perfect vacuum.

2.   **God thinks big.** The universe is at least 93 billion light years across. It contains about 400 billion galaxies and maybe 200 billion trillion stars. (Only about 3000 stars are visible on a good night.) Here we are, inconspicuously circulating around one of them, but what has God cooked up on the other hundreds of billions of trillions? It is hard to feel very special.

3.   **God doesn't rush things** and, indeed, doesn't care much about time. The universe is almost 14 billion years old. And the time we experience can speed up or slow down depending on velocity and gravity and other things.

4.   **God actually likes math.** The creation can be described mathematically. You might even say that math existed before anything else did. Modern physicists find solutions in mathematicians' century-old work.

5.   **God believes in evolution.** God's a change agent. The universe is not a product but an ongoing process. New stars and black holes are being created. Here on Earth, evolution gave rise to life about 3.5 billion years ago, and now, here we humans are, one of evolution's more recent products, busily destroying the place.

**6.   As for salvation, God wants us to save
ourselves.** God is the very opposite of a helicopter
creator, and we are adrift with our own devices. All
of science confirms God is not interfering in human
affairs. We long for angels and miracles, but they are
not to be found in this universe. If there is providence,
we provide it. If there is salvation, we forge it. If love,
we give it.

7.   God likes puzzles, and so left us with some
dillies, like merging quantum theory with relativity, the
early "inflation" of the universe, the possibility of the
multiverse and other worlds, and human nature.

8.   God loves beauty and nature. Just look around,
or listen to God's friend J.S. Bach, or swim among the
corals and blue tang.

9.   God believes in term limits. For starters, we
all die; everything alive dies, even Joshua Trees. Earth
dies, eventually if not before. Our sun has a term limit;
it is slated to die about 4.5 billion years from now.
Most fundamentally, entropy — the inexorable and
vaguely disturbing second law of thermodynamics —
will in due course take care of the whole shebang.

10. God may not be out there at all. We are left
with the biggest question. It is the last question:

Why is there something and not nothing?

The scientist winks and says, "Why not?"

The Way

The way is a path
that leads along the river
under the tall cypress
to a spot where
you can hold hands
and wade into the current
as the dark water flows by
and then heads uphill to
the white pavilion
on the bluff above the river
where the door opens
to a place of memory
and old friends await and smile
on the other side.

A Dog's Life

What do the dogs most enjoy,
other than eating of course?
What do they demand with
wet noses and come-on nudges?

Bright in the mornings,
they chase the ball with
abandon and aplomb.
Proudly, they catch it in the air
and find it lost in the grasses.

It is not the exercise,
nor the praise, but
the sheer joy of accomplishment—
doing what they do well
when they are up for magic.

Later in the day as
boredom creeps in on napping,
they want to explore
the world more slowly.

A walk down the road
and into the woods,
to see where the grouse hide,
to the find some blackberries,
to smell every possible thing,
tails going like metronomes.

Pride in their competence,
joy from their curiosity,
oh, these are just simple animals,
lacking the higher powers.

This Is for the Birds

I have a word feeder,
one heaven fills each day
chock full up with good words
just there for me to say.

I take a word like "hedge."
It makes me think of "row,"
a place the winds are slowed
and where the Brown-head Cowbirds go.

Color words are special.
It is a thrill to get a "red."
I'll use it in Redstart,
but the Redpoll would do instead.

Some words are palindromes —
such as the good old "bob."
It finds a place in Bobolink.
The Bobs are my heartthrob.

Most lovely one of all?
I need to get a "beak."
The Evening Grosbeak was just here
and flew when I let out a shriek.

Getting towards the bottom,
the word I get is "mouse."
(A family of mice once lived
here in my Bluebird house.)
I'm not sure how to best use it,
but then, of course, Titmouse.

Some words are hard to rhyme.
But don't think one is "Wren."
If you get in trouble rhyming,
don't put it at the end!

Generations

I plodded downstairs early this morning
and was sipping a much-needed coffee
when I noticed the yard had more than its
normal complement of robins to see.
These early birds are getting worms, I thought,
worms the heavy rain last night has brought.

I saw something very strange in the yard,
and at that moment our son phoned us.
Char's a busy guy, driving then to work.
There's always family news to discuss.
It's a short drive and is his main time free.
Still, he shares this time with his mom and me.

I listened, but the robins were distracting.
Three were close together, each bird dancing
a quick two-step, moving across the yard.
The largest robin led this prancing
followed closely by two smaller ones —
their triangle hopped around in the sun.

Their movement seemed quite random, but then
the lead bird spotted something by the tree.
She paused while the two trailing birds jumped
quickly to the front, and then there were three
beaks all pecking at the unlucky worm.
My guess this is bird parenting confirmed.

Our son said his daughters have a busy day,
both a soccer game and a hip-hop class.
He'll cover one and his wife the other.
The bird triangle hopped on to new grass.
I thought then how these events well captured
the artistry of lives being nurtured.

Jake and the Flood

We gathered early on that night
toward the end of a sad year
in Jake's old house, not feeling right.

For all, Jake was a man held dear.
A few guests did not want to stay.
The fall's events were still too near.

What was it we could say
in such a place so full of pain?
So there we stood just in the way.

It had all started with the rain.
Then came that knock down wind.
Then came the freaky rains again.

He had long been our friend,
and old enough to be our dad.
For some of them he was their kin.

That dog was mainly what he had.
So when the stream became a torrent,
he ran outside toward her pad.

Tragedy he sought to prevent!
We must celebrate his deep love
and to that love give our assent.

Dear Jake. Found in a downstream cove —
his left arm still holding her tight —
close to the ancient ash tree grove.

The Myth of Sisyphus, by Albert Camus

The gods had condemned Sisyphus
to ceaselessly rolling a rock to the top of a mountain.
From there, the stone would forever fall back of its own weight.
The gods thought there is no more dreadful punishment
than futile and hopeless labor. . . .

His scorn of the gods, his hatred of death, and his passion for life
won him that unspeakable penalty in which
his whole being is exerted toward accomplishing nothing.
This is the price that must be paid for the passions of this earth.

One sees his whole effort straining to raise the huge stone,
to roll it, and push it up a slope a hundred times over;
one sees the face screwed up, the cheek tight against the stone,
the shoulder bracing the clay-covered mass. . . .

At the very end of his long effort,
measured by skyless space and time without depth,
the purpose is achieved.
Then Sisyphus watches the stone rush down
to the lower world from where he will have to push it up again.
He goes back down to the plain.

It is during that return, that pause, that Sisyphus interests me.
A face that toils so close to stones is already stone itself!
I see that man going back down with a heavy yet measured step
toward the torment of which he will never know the end.
That hour, like a breathing-space
which returns as surely as his suffering,
that is the hour of consciousness.

At each of those moments when he leaves the heights
and gradually sinks toward the lairs of the gods,
he is superior to his fate.
He is stronger than his rock.

If this myth is tragic, that is because its hero is conscious.
Where would his torture be, indeed, if at every step
the hope of succeeding upheld him?
Sisyphus, proletarian of the gods, powerless and rebellious,
knows the whole extent of his wretched condition:
it is what he thinks of during his descent.
The lucidity that was to constitute his torture
at the same time crowns his victory.
There is no fate that cannot be surmounted by scorn. …

All Sisyphus' silent joy is contained therein.
His fate belongs to him. Likewise, man
when he contemplates his torment, his absurd condition,
silences all the idols. In the universe suddenly restored to its silence,
the myriad wondering little voices of the earth rise up.
Unconscious, secret calls, invitations from all the faces,
they are the necessary reverse and price of victory.
There is no sun without shadow; it is essential to know the night.
Still, the absurd man says yes.
His efforts will henceforth be unceasing.
He knows himself to be the master of his days.

At that subtle moment, when man glances backward over his life,
Sisyphus returning toward his rock, in that slight pivoting
he contemplates that series of unrelated actions
that become his fate, created by him.
Thus, convinced of the wholly human origin of all that is human,
a blind man eager to see who knows that the night has no end,
he is still on the go. The rock is still rolling.

I leave Sisyphus at the foot of the mountain!
One always finds one's burden again.
But Sisyphus teaches the higher fidelity
that negates the gods and raises rocks.
He concludes that all is well.
This universe, henceforth without a master,
seems to him neither sterile nor futile.
The struggle itself toward the heights is enough to fill a man's heart.
One must imagine Sisyphus happy.

*Adapted slightly by the author from Justin O'Brien's admirable translation
of Albert Camus' The Myth of Sisyphus.*

Sunday Morning

The old man kept his balance
moving across the smooth rocks
on the far bank of the Margaree
along a wide bend in the river.

Since first light he had been
fishing the magnificent river.
The cloak of morning mist,
the feel of his favorite fly rod,
his procession down the swirling water,
the birdsong from the banks,
the salmon pools he knew so well,
it left him feeling renewed, himself.

Over the years he had come
to see the river as close to magic.
His concerns seemed to vanish
when he waded into the water.

Now he was headed for a wooden bench
someone had built long ago
where the river started to curve.
He knew that his dog Jez was lying
by the bench on the warming rocks,
as were the butter tart and hot tea.
Jez's golden color blended with the rocks,
like she was meant to be there.

He felt good about the decades he'd spent
in masonry and construction locally.
He was justified, he reckoned,
by his useful, thoughtful work,
and there had been a lot of that.
But he had made time for fishing,
and he was very glad he had.

It was Sunday and his wife, half jokingly,
had said he should be going to church.
He thought of that as he sat on the bench.
He could still make church if he left now.
But he felt he needed more time with the river.
"You don't have much conflict about it, Jez.
I can see that," he murmured.

He looked up through the tree canopy
to the sky brightening up,
and he thought, not for the first time,
that he was in church already.
He gave a small piece of the tart to Jez,
took a sip of the steaming tea, and
focused down the river where the
sunlight now danced on the water.

The Counsel of Despair

As I navigate among the various faces I have in this world
— the Happy Everyday Me, the Policy Wonk Me, the
New Radical Me — I sometimes stumble to the bottom
and into the Despairing Me. I try not to go there, but
I stumble. In this windowless cellar of my mind, I have
devastating thoughts, not phantasmagoric apparitions
easily dismissed, but thoughts resulting from a calculus
carefully tuned to empirical observation of the world
spanning many years. There, I encounter the thought
that the human enterprise on the planet — ambitious,
arrogant, heedless, at times inspiring — has inadvertently
created an insatiable contraption that is now devouring
the planet at a phenomenal rate and that can no longer
be controlled by human societies. If this contraption
were bringing genuine human satisfaction and wellbeing
while ruining the planet, well, that would be something.
We would at least be going down happy. But as an apt
description of the human condition, I cannot but think
instead of the Tom Lehrer lyric, "The whole world is
festering with unhappy souls." Generally, people are
unhappy for good reason. Some are unhappy because
they are spoiled or misapprehending their circumstances,
but for most there are genuine causes of human misery.
Hard data support deprivations born in economic
disparities, social inequities, environmental decay, political
oppression, invidious discriminations, the failure of
systems of education and health, the loss of community
solidarity and human companionship, and, perhaps most
important, the widespread sense of powerlessness and

hopelessness in the face of these challenges. In this bottom chamber of Despair, that is the ultimate problem: honesty cannot assign a decent probability or even a fighting chance of finding a solution.

Faced with this looming dilemma, human creativity can reach in several directions. First there is Acceptance. One can accept this fate with bitter nihilism or with calm stoicism or, most likely, with hedonistic abandonment. Many will opt, as Thoreau noted, to live lives of quiet desperation and make the best of a bad situation. Second, there is Denial. Denial too can take many directions. One can stick to living in the truthiness world free of fact and science and full of fake reality and mythic beliefs. Or one might believe — and hope! — these problems, like so often in the past, will be solved — somehow, someday, by someone. This is the hopium solution. A third tack, The World Beyond, can be taken by some religious followers who put their faith in the afterlife, not this one. They might welcome climate and other catastrophes as signs of the End Times.

Then, there is the response I will call Rebel and Resist. Here, people fiercely oppose and fight back against their fate, knowing full well it is hopeless but nevertheless rebelling beyond hope because the human spirit tells them with insistence that what is unacceptable — all the suffering, all the loss, all the tears — must not be accepted.

(continued)

Beyond all our fears, it is.
Beyond grieving and crying, it is.
Beyond even hope, it is.
What then is left beyond?

A collapse of sentiment?
What do they feel:
the black man in solitary,
the young girl buried
in the rubble of Aleppo,
the Amazon biologist
watching the forest die?

What do we feel, you and I?
Can the mere knowledge
of the world's desperation
while still in a sheltered space
take us to a place beyond?

I can only speak for myself.
I hunger to strike a blow
so shattering that enthrallment
breaks into a million shards
and falls to the feet of the world.

Moving Through Our Lives

Here's what has kept me going,
and going and going
through these many years.
Maybe you too.

Have you, like me, loved
to learn new things?
The endless search to understand!
Bruner was 95 when asked
why he read long biographies.
"To improve my mind," he said.

What about making things?
People love to build, to create.
The Navajo sand painting blows away.
It is a beautiful thing.
My poems will blow away too.

"Variety is the spice of life"—
one of the smartest things ever said.
People will do anything to
avoid boredom and find excitement.
Trust me on that.

How about comradeship?
We are often casual with friendships,
but a comrade is something special.
Bonding for a good cause!
Comrades inspire us
and keep us going.

Speaking of good causes,
they keep us going too.
Mostly they will fail, but remember
what Camus said of Sisyphus:
"The struggle itself towards the heights
is enough to fill a man's heart.
One must imagine Sisyphus happy."

What's the most important thing of all?
That's a big question. We may differ.
I think it's companionship. What's better!
On the pillow in my wife's chair, it says
"Happiness is being married to your best friend."

I'm carrying on here
too long without getting
down to the serious stuff.
Give us this day our daily sustenance:
the kids and the family,
the dogs and cats and random pets,
the joking and the poking,
the laughing and the hoping,
the cooking and the eating,
all the sublime messes we create!

Then finally, are we the same
in knowing, deep down inside,
that we are close kin to wild things,
and loving that knowing?
I am refreshed when I am
moving in life's intricate web,
pausing in the forest with the dogs,
standing with awe and reverence
in that cathedral of viridescence.

From the Author,
a Note of Appreciation

I am especially happy to have completed this, my fourth book of poems and such. It is my way of trying to say thank you to all those who have helped me along the way and to the many friends who have contributed, knowingly and unknowingly, to my environmental and other efforts.

In this volume, I have not grouped the pieces by theme or otherwise. I hope that in this way each piece will stand on its own. I have, though, interspersed my efforts at humor among the heavier fare, like life itself. I have also included a dozen poems from my earlier volumes because they seem necessary to my story here.

My great appreciation for their contributions here goes to Cece Speth (listed first for ample reason), Anne Pace, Baron Wormser, E.B. Moore, Karim Ahmed, and David Grant, and for their ongoing support and advice, to Sydney Lea, Ina Anderson, Catherine McCullough, Mary Evelyn Tucker, John Grim, Richard Garcia, Jim Antal, Jonathan Stableford, Byron Breese, Megan Mayhew Bergman, Jim Speth, Charles Speth, John Keefe and Martha Manheim. My thank you to all.

It is best to read the three poems on pages 26-31 together. The full story of Sally and Billy, Jonathan and Jennifer, Sam and Molly, Summer, and the admirable Mabel and Merv, who started it all though 1500 miles apart, can be found in *What We Have Instead.*

"What the Preacher Saw" is dedicated to Tom Kinder, and "The Longest History" to Mary Evelyn Tucker and John Grim.

I have reproduced here with only modest adjustments
"The Myth of Sisyphus" by Albert Camus from *The Myth of
Sisyphus and Other Essays* (New York: Vintage Books, 1955),
translated by Justin O'Brien. Also, in "A Nearby Place" I
draw from Sherwood Anderson's endearing *Winesburg, Ohio*
(New York: Penguin Classics, 1992, originally published
in 1919). "The Counsel of Despair" appeared originally in
Orion magazine online, orionmagazine.org/article/counsel-
despair-climate-catastrophe.

I hope you enjoy these efforts!

Gus Speth
Strafford Vermont
Autumn 2022

www.ingramcontent.com/pod-product-compliance
Lightning Source LLC
Chambersburg PA
CBHW031501130726
47989CB00003B/1488

9 798218 101244